WEYK GLOBAL
BOOK SERIES

ZACHARY LUKASIEWICZ

WEYK GLOBAL MEDIA
Lincoln, Nebraska
www.weykglobal.com

Related Courses & Workshops: WeykGlobal.com
LinkedIn: linkedin.com/in/zdrake2013
More about the author: weykglobal.com/leadership
Please send errors, comments, and speaking inquiries to
hey@weykglobal.com

The goal in releasing this book series is to help narrow the gap between professional marketers and industry newcomers. The idea here is to provide necessary information to passionate individuals to make their business dreams a reality. Our marketing materials - including our courses and workshops - are all aligned on this front.

For Whom Is This Book Intended?

This book is meant for start-ups and small businesses that lack marketing-savvy staff but have a need to intelligently expand the reach of their goods or services. These companies may not have the budget to hire external marketing help, and may also find traditional Google tools to be intimidating. We seek to educate and demystify the online marketplace for these organizations.

What Does It Do?

Using a series of lessons, case studies, and quizzes (if you opt for our online courses), this book and its entire series guides you through 3-5 minute story-based chapters on search marketing, content marketing, PR & Media and more. All in all, we cover eighteen different topics. Depending on your sense of humor, our case studies can cause a few chuckles as you think about, for example, how Connor the karaoke rental equipment guy should improve his search results.

The lessons in this book are heavy on strategy and light on execution. Though this book helps readers differentiate between marketing tactics and identify the best strategies for different businesses, it does not go so far as to provide a detailed walk-through of execution using Google tools. That said, it certainly provides enough information to begin taking steps in the right direction.

How Does It Do It?

This book handles dry topics well, making consistency paramount. This keeps readers engaged in the lessons, with no time to lose focus.

Not only highly interactive, the chapters are also very brief at 3-5 minutes. There are also notes about various courses and workshops to help reinforce the takeaways.

Recommending This Book

Reviewing all of the chapters takes less than 45 minutes. As a digital marketing instructor for Growth(X) Academy, I integrate these essentials into my lessons on search marketing and content marketing in order to reinforce concepts.

KEEP YOUR EYES ON THE PRIZE: RUNNING ONLINE GIVEAWAYS

- How can organizing an online giveaway help my marketing?
- How do I run an online giveaway successfully?
- How do I create buzz to promote my online giveaway?

Running an online giveaway in the age of digital media can help you win big with your audience.

That's because people love to get into the spirit of competition. And when people compete or win, they radiate good vibes, which create a warm and fuzzy aura around your brand.

But giveaways do more than generate good vibes from your audience. They can also help you get new customers.

There are 2 main types of giveaways you can run: sweepstakes and contests.

Sweepstakes are like a lottery, and rely purely on chance.

Contests require people to take certain actions to enter, like posting a photo or entering an email address. The winners are determined by vote or other specific judging criteria.

LISTEN UP
Make sure your giveaway is on the legal up-and-up. Laws may vary between states and countries, and from platform to platform.

So before you run the giveaway, you might want to consult with your legal team to make sure there won't be any problems.

No matter what type of giveaway you plan on running, you have to first establish your business goals.

Do you want your giveaway to boost social engagement, generate leads, drive sales, or something else? You might even choose a combination of these goals. Just make your goals clear, as they help you set giveaway rules.

For example, if your goal is generating leads, you can make email addresses an entry requirement. If you want to drive people to your store, you can ask them to upload an in-store photo of themselves to social media and tag their location.

After you've set your goals, you're ready to find a tool that will help you plan and build a giveaway that's right for your brand and target audience.

It's important that the tool you select can support running the giveaway across multiple platforms, especially since so much social media activity happens on mobile.

Campaign-building services like ShortStack, Offerpop, and Stackla can help you build and run giveaways.

Once you've decided which service to use, you'll need to create an externally facing home for your giveaway.

You could create a microsite or devoted page on your website, which will allow people to enter the giveaway, read eligibility rules, and examine the fine-print.

Avoid hosting the giveaway on your social media channels. That's because sometimes there are strict rules about what you can ask people to do on them.

Also, social media channels may limit the type of giveaways you can run, and may make it difficult for people to join in. To help avoid any issues that potentially derail your giveaway, consult with your legal resources.

However, you can usually still use your social media channels to promote your giveaway, provide updates, feature winners, and share giveaway news.

To create buzz around your giveaway, make sure you have the time and resources to run a promotional campaign that leads up to the launch date.

Check if you can promote the giveaway on social media channels. If you can, publish posts about the giveaway on them and in your email newsletters. Also, consider running paid social ads and search and display ads to gain more exposure.

You can also track which social media channels are gaining the most entries by creating a UTM link. It's a custom URL that lets you see which channels or sites people are coming from and how many of them enter the giveaway.

Once the giveaway is underway, promote content that contestants have created and the prizes you're offering across your marketing channels.

When coming up with ideas for prizes, think of ones that are relevant and appropriate for your brand, audience, and the type of giveaway you're running.

If you're asking people to submit something that takes effort or time, make the prize worthwhile. Few will submit a photo of themselves dressed like a chicken for 1 free soda, but they might for a shot at free refills for life.

Along with the grand prizes, consider offering smaller prizes to all contestants. This will make everyone feel like a winner. ("You get a coupon. You get a coupon. Everybody gets a coupon!")

Consider offering special deals like discounts to people who sign up for your newsletter or follow you on social media channels. You can also gain more exposure by letting non-contestants participate in the voting process.

After the giveaway has ended and the winners have been announced, measure how close you are to reaching your business goals.

Compare entries to your existing contact list to see whether the giveaway brought you new leads and if any existing contacts participated. Services like ConstantContact or MailChimp can help you do this.

The benefits of your giveaway can also keep coming as time goes by. A study by digital agency Tamba showed that 84.5% of participants share posts from brands even after the giveaway has ended.

You can run a handful of giveaways a year, but be careful not to overdo it. If you run too many, your audience might stop paying attention.

Remember: Always keep your giveaways legit. Laws and regulation can change over time, and between digital platforms. So make sure you get the thumbs up for your legal sources before running or promoting your giveaway.

DO THIS NOW
Now that you've learned about running online giveaways, let's see if you're ready to make one of your own.

If you're participating in the course, go to the next section to access your self assessment.

KEY TAKEAWAYS
1. Running an online giveaway is a great way to engage your audience, increase brand awareness, collect leads, and drive sales.
2. To get the best results for your efforts, come up with a type of giveaway and prizes that are right for your brand and target audience.

3. Keep your audience engaged by offering special deals, featuring winners, and running several giveaways a year.

SOCIAL AD TACTICS: FOCUS, RESEARCH, MEASURE

- Why should I use social ads to promote my brand?
- How can I set up my social ads for success?
- How do I know if my ads are working?

Imagine Alana's Llamas sells sweaters knit from the wool of – you guessed it – llamas. Alana wants to advertise on social media to let people know she's having a sale.

She isn't quite sure what she wants her ad to say but likes the phrase "Shama-llama-ding-dong" because it's funny and attention-getting. So she uses it as the ad's headline and also features a beautiful photo of a sweater.

She finishes submitting her ad and payment to her chosen social network, closes her laptop, and calls it a day.

You can probably already guess that Alana's social ad won't be hugely effective. Beyond the ad's headline, where did Alana go wrong?

Done right, social media ads (AKA those display ads and promoted posts on social networks) can help you efficiently connect with your target audience.

That's because social media ads let you reach audiences based on occupation, interests, locations, gender, and other information people like to share on social networks.

These ads also let you measure how effective they are, kind of like a built-in self-evaluation function. You can track how many leads the ads bring in and/or how many people sign-up or take other actions based on your call to action (CTA).

To get the most out of your social media ads, however, set them up and run them strategically. Research your target audience, set a goal, develop and test your ads' creative elements, and measure your ROI.

First, let's look at setting goals for your social ads. You don't want to leave your ads stranded on a social network without a specific job to do.

Decide on the one thing you want each ad to help you do. Do you want newsletter signups? Social media followers? More sales? Don't forget: Your ads' visuals, messaging, and call to action (CTA) need to drive to this goal.

Whatever your goal is, make it the one and only focus of that ad. Giving your ad too many jobs to accomplish and your audience too many CTA's to choose from can hurt your ad's performance.

Next, research your target audience. Beyond looking at demographics, make sure you're targeting the right audiences by checking out similar businesses.

Specifically, look at who you want to follow you on platforms like Twitter and LinkedIn. Then set up ads to target those people.

Also, not every social platform is right for your brand and goals. Invest your time and money on the ones that are most popular with your audience and that get you the best ROI.

To figure out where you should be investing, analyze your website data to determine which social media channels are driving traffic your way. Tools like Google Analytics and Adobe Analytics can help you do this.

You can also go through the process of creating an ad on a social platform without actually buying or running the ad. This can give you valuable insights into the targeting capabilities of that particular platform.

REMEMBER
Good results aren't just about getting a high click-through rate.

You want to invest in social platforms that have audiences who engage with your brand and also complete your ad's CTA.

Knowing your target audience and your social media platforms will help you develop and test your ads' creative elements.

To come up with the right message, check your brand's social media pages for your most popular non-paid posts. Study their language, tone of voice, and content, and use what worked well to help you craft your ads (as long as it's relevant to your goal).

Messaging should be goal-oriented and also clearly state the benefits of clicking on your ad (like "30% off"). You pay per click, so you want to avoid click-throughs where people leave your site right away because it's not what they expected.

Your visuals should stay true to your branding and imagery your customers are familiar with. If your ad leads to a landing page on your website, make sure the visuals on both match.

TOOLS
To track the performance of your creative elements, use third-party analytics tools like Marketo or Salesforce to monitor ads and test variations.

This lets you be more hands-on with tracking, versus relying solely on social platforms' analytics.

Once your ads are up and running, it's time to measure your ROI – or how effectively and efficiently your ads are helping you reach your goal.

If your goal is conversions or sales, a good ROI means you make more from your social ads than you spend on them. To track which site customers came from social ads, you can use UTM-coded URLs (trackable text added onto your site URL).

Some social platforms also offer pixel tracking programs, where you embed snippets of code that let you see how people are interacting with your ads.

If your goal is generating leads, you can assess your ROI by figuring out your cost of acquisition, or how much each lead is worth to your business. To get this information, you first need to calculate your average conversion rate.

Let's say you know 4 out of every 100 people who visit your website (leads) end up buying (conversions), and they spend an average of $1,000. Your average conversion rate is 4%, or 4 conversions ÷ 100 leads.

To get your cost of acquisition, take the average conversion rate and multiply it by customers' average spend. In our example, it would be 4% x $1000, which is $40. For a good ROI, then, your social ads need to cost less than this per lead.

DO THIS NOW
You may be pretty far along in the social ads process, or you may be just starting out. Let's do a quick, no-pressure assessment to figure out your next steps.

If you're participating in the course, go to the next section to access your self assessment.

KEY TAKEAWAYS
1. Social ads are an efficient and trackable way to target your audience.
2. You should choose one business goal for your ads and research your target audience and social platforms.

3. Have a plan in place to measure your ads' messaging and visuals, as well as your ROI.

WORK WITH SOCIAL MEDIA INFLUENCERS TO SELL MORE

- What are social media influencers?
- How can they help my brand?
- How can I engage with them?

Imagine there's a new company called Rough Links that sells cuff links decorated with unpolished gems and stones.

Rough Links has had early success with a small, loyal customer base, but they're hoping to reach a larger audience.

Rough Links knows they sell the majority of their cuff links to fashion-forward men in their twenties. They also know that this audience is active on social media and men's style blogs.

With this in mind, they start brainstorming ways to convince potential customers that Rough Links is an authentic brand that sells unique, high-quality cuff links. Let's see which idea works best.

Now imagine there's a men's fashion blogger named Fritz Glitz who has a popular website and a sizable social media following.

Rough Links thinks they could get new customers if Fritz Glitz wrote about them, so they reach out and send him several free pairs of cuff links. They also offer to do a cross promotion where Fritz Glitz writes a series of posts on the Rough Links blog.

Fritz Glitz had never heard of Rough Links, but when he tries their products, he falls in love with the brand. He posts pictures of himself wearing their cuff links on his social media platforms and agrees to write for the Rough Links website.

Fritz Glitz's posts get 20,000+ likes and help Rough Links reach half a million potential customers. New orders start rolling in. Fritz Glitz gets some new fans, in addition to the free cuff links. Everyone wins.

Social media influencers are bloggers, celebrities, experts, and others who have a big impact on online (and offline) culture.

Because of their social clout, social media influencers can be valuable to your brand and marketing. After all, they often come with tens of thousands of followers who actively follow them and respect their opinions.

An endorsement from an influencer can add an extra layer of authenticity to your brand, and help people relate to your products and services on a more personal level.

That can build your brand's awareness, trust, and favorability, and give your social media following a nice, lead-generating boost.

LISTEN UP
70% of people say they want to learn about products through online content versus traditional ads.

That means social media marketing via influencers can be a powerful strategy.

So, influencers sound great. How do you figure out which ones to engage? Start by figuring out how your brand fits into the social media landscape.

Look at the brand category you're in (cooking, lifestyle, cars, tech, design, etc.) and check which social media platforms your target audience is most active on.

Then research which influencers your audience is already following, and make a list of the most prominent ones who are also in your brand category. Larger brands might approach this step differently than smaller brands.

If you're a larger brand, you might use a digital agency that specializes in sourcing influencers with a global reach. If you're a smaller brand, you might want to use services like Klout to help you assess influencers who have a local following.

Evaluate these influencers' social media content. Would it appeal to your entire target audience? How much do their followers match your current audience? How large are their followings on your chosen social media platforms?

Also, consider if their content is right for your brand. What kind of reach/exposure do their articles and posts get? Have you interacted with them before? Have they mentioned your brand or products in the past?

TIP
Once you're ready to engage with influencers, get on their radar before jumping into offers and negotiations. Basically, be social on social media: Share the influencers' posts, photos, Tweets, or other content. (And don't forget to tag them or give them shout outs in your reposts.)

After you've made yourself known to an influencer by engaging with them, you're ready to get in touch.

There are different ways you can do this, including messaging them directly through their social media channels, looking for contact information on their website, or finding a mutual contact who can connect you.

Also, if you've previously interacted with the influencer and they're already familiar and comfortable with your brand, you can ask for their direct contact information and take the conversation offline.

Ideally, influencers you contact will be interested in your products. If you're a smaller brand, approaching influencers with a large following might be unrealistic. Find influencers whose follower count is more within your ballpark.

And remember, there are laws and regulations that apply to endorsement or influencer campaigns, so you may want to consult with your legal department before getting started.

DO THIS NOW
Are you ready to engage with social media influencers? Let's find out with a quick self-evaluation.

If you're participating in the course, go to the next section to access your self assessment.

KEY TAKEAWAYS
1. Social media influencers are bloggers, celebrities, and experts with a large amount of followers who trust their opinion.
2. An endorsement from an influence can help your brand appear now authentic and relatable.
3. Once you've found the right influencers, get in touch by messaging them directly or finding a mutual contact who can connect you.

SURVIVING AND THRIVING ON SOCIAL MEDIA

- Why do I need a social media strategy?
- What should I think about when I post?
- How can I define my voice?

Using social media to market your business seems pretty straightforward. You just post, get the word out, and wait for new customers.

But there's actually a lot more to it. Every single one of your posts should be part of a larger social media strategy. For example, let's say there's a new restaurant called Pete's Paleo Pizza that sells gluten-free, dairy-free pizza.

Pete just set up some social media accounts to market his pizza and is eager to start posting and gaining new followers. But how can he make sure he's actually helping his business when he posts?

Doing social media right is like hosting a successful dinner party. It's your job to keep the chatter flowing and fun, while also creating a welcoming atmosphere.

Being a party host takes a solid plan, an open mind, and close attention to the wants and needs of your guests. The same goes for running an effective social media account.

The 4 things you should pay attention to while doing social

media are voice, content, timing, and conversation. Let's explore all of them in more detail.

You should shape your voice and presence around your audience. To do this, you should get to know them.

What are their interests? Where do they live? What do they do? What places (or other social media sites) do they visit?

If you forget everything else, remember this: If you know your audience, you can find your voice. If you find your voice, you can reach your audience.

Think of your content as the furniture in your house. It should represent your taste, generate conversation, and keep a consistent style throughout.

Your content should also make people feel comfortable. Social media is all about getting your audience to communicate with you and feel good in your presence.

That means: Don't use social media solely as a place to sell yourself or your product. Use it to tell your story, connect with your audience, and portray a feeling.

Take your audience behind the scenes of your business, share news and events, and post how-to's and photos. Ask people for their opinions and acknowledge holidays, birthdays, and special occasions. All of this can help build customer loyalty.

There's a fine line between engaging your audience and overloading them. That's why timing is so important in social media.

Posting off-schedule or twice in a row is fine sometimes, but just make sure to keep a good balance (AKA cadence). Don't bombard your audience with content, but don't go silent, either.

1 or 2 posts per platform each day should do it – at hours when your audience is most active, of course. For Pete, this might be in the morning, after his Paleos' daily run, and at lunchtime, while

they're eating kale at their desks.

Finally, remember that the conversation isn't all about you. Get to know your audience – they're your focus group. Ask questions. Start discussions. Respond.

Feel free to give a little push with a call to action. This is a fancy term for telling your audience to do something... like asking them to submit relevant photos and stories or sending them to your website when you're having a sale.

Yes, we used the "S" word. It's okay to drive sales through your social media sometimes. But in order to do that, you've got to entertain your customers, too.

TIP
The best thing about social media is that it lets you interact with almost anyone directly. Bloggers, experts, even celebrities are at your fingertips. Reach out to them to increase your presence. And when one of them writes about you, be sure to reshare their post and tag them.

Let's see how General Electric (GE) used social media to transform their business.

GE used social media to change their brand from one that only meant "appliances" to one that brings innovation and technology to mind.

First, they defined their target audience: forward-thinking, innovative, and interested in health, transportation, and the infrastructure of their cities. To reach this audience, GE developed a playful yet educational voice.

For posts, GE used eye-catching images, videos, links, and questions. For example, they would share photos of their scientists working on robots, which showed both the technical and human sides of the company.

GE's content also always hits one of these topics: end benefits (how GE's products have helped build a better world), the employees at GE, and success stories of how GE's innovation has touched people's lives.

By using a strong, consistent voice and by making their social media not solely about their products, GE's content became the center of a new global conversation.

DO THIS NOW
Now that you've learned what goes into a social media presence, you can start defining your voice.

If you're participating in the course, go to the next section to access your self assessment.

KEY TAKEAWAYS
1. To know your voice, you must first know you're audience.
2. Keep a consistent tone to build connection with your audience.
3. Voice, content, timing, and community are the building blocks of a social media strategy.

WEYK GLOBAL LEADERSHIP

Zachary Lukasiewicz is the Managing Director of Weyk Global.

Originally from Omaha, Nebraska and attended Drake University in Des Moines, Iowa. He served as a tri-chair for the Human Capital committee of Capital Crossroads, the 10-year plan for Central Iowa, where he focused on the attraction and retention of Des Moines residents from cradle to career.

Zachary has operated 50+ accelerator assistance programs and in-house workshops, and staffed marketing teams around the globe.

Zachary's focus is marketing investment - sourcing the best talent, recruiting domain experts and executing on his proven playbook and delivering the best possible experience. He sets the strategic direction and client profile within the program, including a curated team of mentors, investors and business advisors.

Zachary is responsible for making the initial relationships. He takes overall ownership of each programs' success and partners with other operations units external to Weyk Global to ensure exceptional delivery of exceptional marketing programs, and is ultimately responsible for turning good companies into great ones.

Additional:

• Builds systems around market research and data-driven management—especially in budget allocation, paid/organic, and navigating complex customer cadences.
• Experience building marketing infrastructure and communication processes throughout US Techstars classes, reducing acquisition costs with greater capacity and cost-effectiveness
• A recognized expert on US social media in real estate, education, and human resources industries
• A leader with proven skills working with innovative teams to build customer consensus and drive buy-in behavior across purpose-driven organizations
• Motivates large organizations and individual personnel to award-winning performance and achievement
• Leadership experience encompasses direct management of 20+ personnel, over $8.5 million in assets/budgets with a record of five enterprise acquisitions and assisting in seven fundraising rounds

Zachary has served as a management consultant with startups backed by White Star Capital, Hoxton Ventures, Bloomberg Beta, Real Ventures, BDC Capital, Chris Anderson. Eduardo Gentil, Jacqueline Novogratz, Mehdi Alhassani, Ana Carolina, Entrepreneur, Obvious Ventures, MIT, Ittleson Foundation, J.M.Kaplan Fund, SC/E, MassCEC, WhiteHouse.gov, ServiceCorps, The One Foundation, The Godley Family Foundation, the Boston Foundation, Boris Jabes, Ilya

Sukhar, Chris DeVore, Alex Payne, DJF, Liquid 2 Ventures, GSF, Sanjay Jain, Felix Anthony, Uma Raghavan, and TiE LaunchPad. Zachary's early experience comes from working under business leaders at market-leading companies including ISoft Data Systems, LukeUSA, AlphaPrep.net, Staffing Nerd, Immun.io, Reflect.io, Validated.co, Shaun White Enterprises, Solstice.us, Swym, Staffing Robot, Hatchlings, Coaching Actuaries, 8 to Great, Target, Paylease, MidAmerican Energy, and R&R Realty Group.

Weyk Global offers two types of in-house training:

- Our workshops at any location:
All advertised courses can be taught in the location of your choice at a time convenient for you. We will ensure the course is specific to your business and sector.

- Our workshops tailored to your needs:
We can design bespoke training to meet the needs of your business. You can provide a brief or we will work with you to develop the training resources to help you achieve your goals.

Analytics Fundamentals

Discover the fundamentals of analytics and the different tools that will help you draw insights from analytics.

In this workshop, we'll examine the fundamentals of analytics, exploring the tools and their most appropriate use. You'll discover how to draw insights from analytics, enabling you to predict emerging trends. This course is designed for those who are curious in nature, enjoy problem-solving and prefer a self- learning, exploratory approach to knowledge.

Career Accelerator

Ensure you have the skills and knowledge to quickly start making an impact in your organization.

Getting into the industry is always challenging; university provides many of the concepts but not necessarily all the skills to be really ready to make a difference. This workshop enables junior marketers to be successful sooner, by understanding the basic concepts and platforms of their day-to-day jobs and getting the skills they need to become more effective in their roles.

Content Marketing Strategy

Examine all areas of content marketing and the role they play in digital, marketing and business strategies.

Best-practice case studies will walk you through all the components of an effective content strategy. You'll also focus on how to create, distribute and manage your content.

Consumers prefer to be engages with a brand via a story or conversation, so the power of content is immeasurable. Through both in-class discussion and practical exercises, we'll explore how consumer behavior fuels this power and how you can develop your content marketing strategy to be just as powerful. You'll also learn how to properly measure its effectiveness.

Conversion Rate Optimization

Harness the power of conversion and learn how to optimize your site to achieve your online objectives.

This powerful workshop will teach you the fundamentals of how to turn your hard-earned website visitors into leads and sales. Applying the insights you'll get will help you improve your conversion rates leading to increased online revenue and lead generation. If you want to know more about the fast-growing marketing discipline of conversion rate optimization, this is the best workshop for you to dip your toe in the water and get started.

Copywriting (Advanced)

Explore new, clever and engaging ways to push your writing to the next level.

Writing today is an indispensable skill and if you want to excel, you need more than just the basics. Throughout this workshop, you'll engage with and produce strategic and compelling copy that will attract readers.

Copywriting (Essentials)

Discover the essential techniques for writing effective copy.

One of our most popular workshops, copywriting essentials explores the structure, rules and techniques in copywriting. Learn to craft compelling headlines, structure documents and most importantly, engage your reader.

Copywriting for Content Marketing

Plan, write and publish creative content that engages readers and keeps them coming back for more.

During this course, you'll explore copywriting for blogs, PR, social media posts and articles. Discover new techniques and master traditional ones. Explore a variety of effective, compelling and fresh techniques for copywriting for content marketing during this hands-on workshop.

Creative Leadership

Develop senior creative leadership skills to improve business effectiveness.

Winning the promotion and becoming a senior manager

doesn't mean you are ready for all that is ahead of you as you take on more responsibility and manage a team or sets of teams. Becoming a good leader in the new digital economy is not an easy task as there are many opportunities and challenges to tackle every single day. This course will help develop a creative culture, nurture creative talent, help build trusted business relationships that allow you and others to succeed and link business and creative needs with technology and innovation.

Customer Journey Mapping

Ensure customer understanding is at the heart of your marketing.

Create a compelling experience for customers using analytics tools and insights. Customer insights are a crucial part of any marketing strategy or campaign, and yet most marketing strategies are developed with a focus on the product attributes or benefits we want to communicate. In this course, you'll discover the fundamentals of analytics and the different tools that will help you draw insights from data to create a compelling customer experience.

CX for CMOs

This workshop brings together all the critical pieces you need to know in the age of information excess.

CX is not one thing, it's every way the customer experiences your brand and business. This workshop, curated by CMOs, brings together all of the critical pieces that are demanded of CMOs today in delivering customer experience - the holy grail of marketing – giving you real clarity on how to apply these insights to your business.

Data Analytics for Marketers

Engage with data analysis and discover how it can deliver

marketing effectiveness.

This short workshop will help you make sense of the high volume and increasingly complex data available to marketers, as well as build a high-level view of the tools, techniques and processes you might use in the process.

Data Driven Marketing Leadership

Broaden your skill set as a leader and develop a data-driven marketing mindset to support your technical team leaders.

During this workshop, you'll be provided with an outline of how business operations and governance work within the field of data, how to lead and inspire your technical teams and to provide cross-functional management and integration.

Data Driven Marketing Practitioner

Learn how to use data to drive your business forward.

In this workshop, we'll show you how to access both primary and third-party data, develop actionable insights, explore data research and perform analytical techniques. This will help you to tell stories with data, benchmark insights from analytics and incorporate the latest solutions and models to tackle business problems. Our Data-driven Practitioner Workshop is designed for those who have access to data directly and/or who have a team and prefer a self-learning, exploratory approach to learning.

Data Driven Marketing Strategy

Discover how a data-driven marketing strategy can deliver a successful customer-centric marketing presence.

In this workshop, we examine a more strategic approach to using your data. This allows us to uncover information about how customers interact with your brand and identify areas that would otherwise go undetected.

Data Visualization

Establish your own visualization techniques that will help sell your analytics results to business decision makers.

In this workshop, you'll learn how to translate and present analytics in an enticing manner. You'll draw upon insights from data and convert these into commercial insights. This workshop is designed for those who are curious in nature, enjoy problem-solving and prefer a self-learning, exploratory approach to knowledge.

Digital Analytics for Marketers

Introducing an accessible approach to measuring, analyzing and optimizing digital marketing activity.

Learn to apply proven marketing theories to real world examples. Unlock the power of data to enhance decision making and campaign planning. This workshop has been designed so a difficult topic is now simple, straightforward and easy to grasp.

Digital Copywriting Essentials

Discover the essential skills and practices for writing effective digital copy.

Whether it's a quick status update or detailed blog post, writing on a digital platform is already a part of your day. The structures and styles for online are, however, different - there is no one-size-fits-all approach to different platforms. For your copy to cut through the current cluttered digital environment, it needs to be engaging. Through tested techniques, you'll discover the art of writing engaging digital copy for search purposes, emails, websites and social media.

Digital Marketing Campaign Planning & Management

Broaden your skills base by discovering how digital can make your campaigns thrive.

During this workshop, you'll explore the practical elements of digital marketing and how you can integrate them within your brand's activity. You'll learn to determine the right resources, budget, plan and identify opportunities for optimization.

Digital Marketing Channels

Discover how each digital marketing channel can deliver you a customer-centric marketing presence.

In this workshop, we examine each channel individually and uncover information about channel contributions to the consumer journey and how to utilize it in your marketing activity.

Digital Marketing Essentials

Discover industry tips and tricks for successfully incorporating digital channels into your campaigns.

In this two-day intensive workshop, you'll explore the foundations of each digital channel, how they work and how they can fit together to deliver on your marketing objectives. We'll also look at digital tactics, strategies and processes and how you can tie them all together in an effective way.

Digital Marketing Foundations

Broaden your skill set and develop a foundational knowledge of the digital landscape, data, content and customer experience.

During this workshop you'll be provided with an outline of the core foundations and principles of digital marketing. Explore the role of data and content and how this can shape customer experience.

Digital Marketing Strategy

Uncover a framework for successful digital marketing.

Whether it's your business, industry, or campaign, digital continues to have a significant impact on the way we operate. During this workshop, you'll be provided with a framework for crafting a digital marketing strategy. To get the most out of this two-day intensive workshop, you should have a good understanding of the basic digital marketing tactics.

Email Marketing

Boost your email marketing results with proven techniques, technical and strategy improvements.

Explore new ways of using email marketing in your overall communications strategy and learn how to deploy marketing automation techniques to drive customer engagement.

Practical Predictive Analytics

Develop a deeper understanding of predictive analytics.

Using predictive analytics, discover how you can forecast, model and optimize data to create opportunities and prevent loss. To get the most out of this course, you should have a solid knowledge of analytics and have ideally spent some time working in the field - over three years' experience is recommended.

Privacy & Marketing Compliance

A commercial approach to compliance for data-driven marketers and advertisers.

Learn how to protect and enhance your brand's reputation by ensuring your marketing and advertising meets customer expectations and complies with the privacy and marketing content laws.

Programmatic Advertising

Adopt a simple, fresh and effective platform to power your marketing.

Programmatic advertising is reshaping the digital landscape as it's automating everything. Marketers need to exploit the power of automated media trading and learn how they can optimize its productivity. In this workshop, we'll explore various programmatic models and the different technologies available for implementation.

Retention & Loyalty Marketing Strategy

Discover the four pillars to building a comprehensive customer retention and loyalty marketing strategy.

In this two-day intensive workshop, you'll adopt a framework for retaining customers through loyalty marketing strategies. We'll explore the power behind loyalty and advocacy initiatives in both traditional and digital techniques. The proven effectiveness of keeping a customer and nurturing their loyalty and advocacy is where the value is derived.

SEM Essentials

Simple yet successful ways to enhance your search results.

Paid search can transform your business without a huge spend. It's a cost effective, highly convenient channel. See how it can strengthen your search engine marketing, morph into a wider digital strategy for your business and leverage other channels.

Sentiment Analysis

Discover best-practice approaches that use modern text mining and predictive analytics techniques to gain insight into consumer opinions and forecast behaviors.

In this course, you'll advance your knowledge of sentiment and content analysis, and opinion mining, develop a deeper understanding of how to work with unstructured text data (in particular, data retrieved from social media) and learn how traditional machine learning/predictive analytics techniques can be used for the purposes of sentiment analysis. It is recommended that you complete the Practical Predictive Analytics Workshop prior to taking this workshop. This workshop is designed for those who are curious in nature, enjoy problem solving and prefer a self-learning, exploratory approach to knowledge.

SEO Essentials

Find out how SEO drives new customers and better customer engagement.

Score page rankings, better click-throughs, utilize research tools and foster great external links with an effective SEO strategy. Discover what simple techniques can do when applied to your website structure.

Social Media Marketing Essentials

Discover the foundations behind social media marketing and how you can adopt the practices into your own communications mix.

Get up to speed with the latest trends, techniques and technologies in social media and learn to craft your own social media campaign through planning, execution and optimization.

Social Media Marketing Strategy

Research, plan and implement a successful social media marketing strategy from the ground up.

Most organizations and brands are on social media - and if they're not, they should be. Social media is a way for consumers to engage and communicate with brands. But this doesn't mean businesses should just start a Facebook page or Twitter account. It's not that simple, as there are right and wrong strategies to use with each channel. Looking at these channels and their tactics, you'll learn how to develop, implement and measure social media activity.

Community & Customer Relationship Management

- Do you need help improving the efficiency and effectiveness of your marketing management?
- Do you have sufficient time and resources to create and distribute resources to your industry and customer base?
- Are your outreach efforts stagnant or causing disruptions to operations?
- Do you have a potential conflict of interest by handling your on-going marketing programs with operational resources?

Global Help Desk & Support

- Do you support customers globally, but lack in-house bandwidth and expertise?
- Do you struggle to quantify the value of your marketing program?
- Are you tired of getting blamed for missed opportunities or slow response times?
- Do you have trouble tracking, prioritizing and resolving requests for support?

Marketing Automation Enablement

- Having trouble identifying or selecting marketing automation solutions?
- Do you want more out of your current go-to-market solution?
- Are you in need of consistent communication with your customers?
- Do you lack the budget for technology, but wish you could leverage technology without a capital investment?

Pre-Post M&A Support: Marketing Bridge

- Are you involved in the pre-acquisition due diligence process and concerned with successor liability?
- Do you lack bandwidth or expertise to integrate, oversee or transition a newly acquired company into your marketing program?
- Are you struggling to address customer acquisition risks identified during due diligence?

Agency of Record

- Do you want to grow your marketing team, but lack the budget?
- Do you wish you could leverage the best in industry digital marketing talent without sacrificing equity?
- Are you looking to create a narrative for potential business expansion?
- Do you want access to modular marketing growth without committing to multi-year contracts?

Opportunity Identification & Innovation Management

- Do you need help analyzing the potential savings and benefits from potential customer or product line expansion?
- Do you wish you had time to qualify marketing tools or implement a baseline for business growth?
- Do you have a go-to-marketing plan in place, but lack the staff to manage your day-to-day?

Third Party Vendor Management

- Do you lack the time or resources to audit and ensure your marketing vendors' quality and service performance level?
- Are you tired of correcting errors or performing your vendors' responsibilities?
- Are you unknowingly putting your Company's reputation and compliance at risk by relying on incorrect best practices and roadmap?
- When was the last time you audited your vendor's fees or timeliness of deliveries?

Marketing Program Optimization

- When was the last time you assessed your Company's marketing-related risks, gaps, and challenges?
- Do your processes and procedures reflect your current business requirements and risk tolerance?
- Is your staff configured to support a major marketing migration

www.ingramcontent.com/pod-product-compliance
Lightning Source LLC
LaVergne TN
LVHW041222050326
832903LV00021B/746